SUPER SNAKES

PYTHON

Murray "Oak" Tapeta

NORWOOD HOUSE PRESS

Cataloging-in-Publication Data

Names: Tapeta, Murray.
Title: Python / Murray Tapeta.
Description: Buffalo, NY : Norwood House Press, 2026. | Series: Super snakes | Includes glossary and index.
Identifiers: ISBN 9781978575134 (pbk.) | ISBN 9781978575141 (library bound) | ISBN 9781978575158 (ebook)
Subjects: LCSH: Pythons--Juvenile literature.
Classification: LCC QL666.O67 T374 2026 | DDC 597.96'78--dc23

Published in 2026 by
Norwood House Press
2544 Clinton Street
Buffalo, NY 14224

Designer: Rhea Magaro
Editor: Kim Thompson

Photo credits: Cover, p. 1 Mark_Kostich/Shutterstock.com; p. 3 kavram/Shutterstock.com; p. 4 EPDICAY/Shutterstock.com; p. 5 Lauren Suryanata/Shutterstock.com; p. 6 Kurit afshen/Shutterstock.com; p. 7dwi putra stock/Shutterstock.com; pp. 8, 9 Yatra4289/Shutterstock.com; p. 9 Ali lyoob Photography/Shutterstock.com; p. 10 chomplearn/Shutterstock.com; p. 11 Decha Photography/Shutterstock.com; p. 12 Ken Griffiths/Shutterstock.com; p. 13Jack911/Shutterstock.com; p. 14 Wirestock Creators/Shutterstock.com; p. 15 Padodo/Shutterstock.com; p. 17 Gulliver20/Shutterstock.com; pp. 18, 19 Sriram Bird Photography/Shutterstock.com; p. 19 Villiers Steyn/Shutterstock.com; p. 20 Vince Adam/Shutterstock.com; p. 21 NickEvansKZN/Shutterstock.com;

Printed in the United States of America

CPSIA compliance information: Batch #CSNHP26: For further information contact Norwood House Press at 1-800-237-9932.

TABLE OF CONTENTS

What Is Special about Pythons?

Pythons are some of the largest, most powerful snakes in the world. They are not poisonous. They have no **venom**. A python kills by squeezing its prey to death.

Pythons live longer than most snakes. A ball python at the St. Louis Zoo lived to be 62 years old!

What Do Pythons Look Like?

There are more than 40 different python **species**. Pythons are often green, brown, or yellow. They can change color as they age.

Most pythons have **markings**. A Burmese python has reddish-brown blotches. It has an arrow-shaped pattern on its head.

Pythons are giant snakes. Some reticulated pythons can be 32 feet (10 meters) long. That is longer than a three-story building is tall.

A python can unfold its jaw. This makes its big mouth even bigger. It allows the snake to swallow big prey.

Where Do Pythons Live?

Pythons are often kept as pets. Wild pythons live in Africa, Asia, and Australia. They can be found in forests, swamps, and grassy **savannas**.

The green tree python rests on tree branches. It dangles its tail to attract prey.

How Do Pythons Hunt?

Young pythons eat every few days. Older, larger pythons can go weeks between meals. Hungry pythons hunt during the night or day.

Pythons look for rodents, birds, and lizards. Big pythons also hunt **mammals** like pigs, antelope, monkeys, and **wallabies**.

Pythons are **ambush** hunters. They strike at prey from a hiding place. After they bite, they do not let go.

Pythons do not have fangs like other snakes. Instead, they have over 100 small, sharp, **recurved** teeth.

A python quickly wraps its body around prey. It **constricts** the animal until it stops breathing. Then, it swallows the meal whole.

Other animals hunt pythons. Young pythons get eaten by large insects, spiders, and other snakes.

Hawks, falcons, and other birds of prey use their talons to capture and kill pythons.

How Do Pythons Reproduce?

Most pythons lay eggs once a year. The female **coils** herself around the eggs until they hatch. If it gets cold, she shivers to keep the eggs warm.

South African python mothers protect babies for a short time after they are born. After two weeks, the young pythons are on their own.

Glossary

ambush (AM-bush): attacking from a hiding place

coils (koilz): wraps up into a series of loops

constricts (kuhn-STRIKTS): squeezes or tightens

mammals (MAM-uhlz): animals that are warm-blooded, that have hair or fur, that usually give birth to live babies, and that produce milk to feed their babies

markings (MAHRK-ingz): colored lines, shapes, or patterns on the surface of something

recurved (REE-kurvd): curved backward or inward

savannas (suh-VAN-uhz): flat, grassy plains with few or no trees

species (SPEE-seez): groups of similar living things that can reproduce with each other

venom (VEN-uhm): a toxic substance that is produced by an animal to harm or kill prey and enemies

wallabies (WAH-luh-beez): small Australian animals related to kangaroos

Thinking Questions

1. On what continents do pythons live?
2. What is special about a python's jaws and mouth?
3. What do pythons eat?
4. How does a python kill prey?
5. How often do pythons lay eggs?

Index

About the Author

Murray "Oak" Tapeta was born in a cabin without plumbing in Montana. Growing up in the great outdoors, he became a lover of nature. He earned the nickname "Oak" after climbing to the top of an oak tree at the age of three. Oak loves to read and write. He has written many books about events in history and other subjects that fascinate him. He prefers spending time in the wilderness with his dog Birchy.